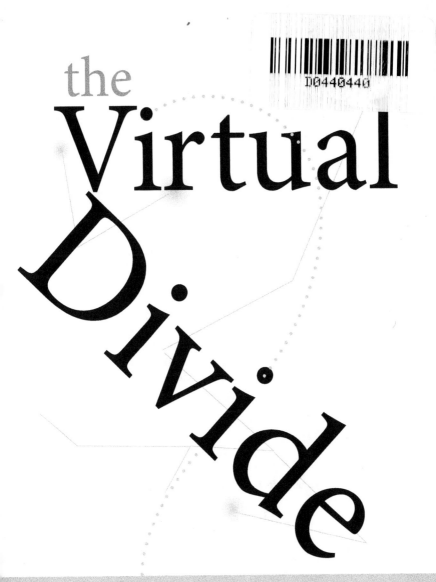

the Virtual Divide

Tackling Your Challenges of Leading in a Virtual World

Ronald B. Beach

VIRTUAL NUGGETS SERIES

Virtual Publishing, LLC
For discounts for bulk orders, contact the publisher at:
VirtualPublishing@gmail.com
15934 Elizabeth Street
Thorton, Colorado 85934

Cover and Interior Design: Rebecca Finkel, FPGD.com
eBook Conversion: Rebecca Finkel, FPGD.com
Book Consultant and Editor: Judith Briles, TheBookShepherd.com

ISBN paperback: 978-1-947746-00-8
ISBN eBook: 978-1-947746-01-5
ISBN audio book: 978-1-947746-02-2

Library of Congress Control Number: 2018906787

Business, Communications,
Management, Leadership

CONTENTS

To the Virtual Divide

Ron Beach has written a very lively book to which I am delighted to respond with a Foreword. *The Virtual Divide* contains an amazing range of tips on how to succeed as a leader or, for that matter, as an effective manager.

Virtual teams are of course more challenging to run than teams where all its members are present. The advantage of actually meeting with people is that we can gauge their reactions by assessing their level of attention. It soon becomes plain what people think about what others are contributing. Useful contributors are welcome and sure to be invited again. That is how one learns about whether one person has a useful role in a team. In other cases, it may be that a person would fit better in a position where individual decision making offers more scope. I think that the cardinal issue makes the case for arranging face-to-face meetings, periodically or occasionally, for virtual teams to ensure that everyone is happy about how the team is operating.

When it comes to the subject of team leadership, there is always one issue that needs to be borne in mind. I have found from experience that the very word *leadership* can be a magnet to those who believe that a course with such a title offers a quick route into seniority and a higher salary. In reality, *team leadership* is more about sharing power and decision-making. The good news is that mastery of skills in this area is excellent preparation for promotion into senior positions in management. The rule seems to be the higher a position, the more complex issues become. This is where complementary skills and team roles work so well when working in conjunction.

Learning about the team roles for which a person is best suited can, in any case, prove of great value in life generally. I have just one final cautionary point to make. How others assess a person's team role profile is of equal importance as to how the self sees the self. A good fit denoted authenticity. A poor fit can mean everyone is misled including the self. It is worth getting to grips with the subject. And I know Ron Beach will help you.

So, go to it, and get the best from the learning.

—Meredith Belbin
Cambridge, England

CHAPTER 1

THE VIRTUAL WORK WORLD ... YOU LOVE IT ... AND HATE IT!

Today's work world is different.
Workers are different. Employers are different.
And expectations are different from leadership,
management, employees, and customers.

Kyle is stressed and grasping the end of his desk in frustration.

What the hell is going go?
What am I doing wrong?
Why can't I connect with them?

His stress meter is picking up. He has countless meetings and phone calls with manufacturing management in Wichita and Ireland to tackle supply problems with materials coming from China. The morning started with answering emails from the boss in California—*does this guy ever sleep?*—followed with conference calls between engineering groups in Denver and Boston to brainstorm a new product introduction.

If he is like 80% of new managers, he received no training on how to manage virtual groups. Kyle is a new supervisor facing the issue of how to manage an expanding virtual organization by blending technology with his leadership skills. It's no wonder that he starts off mentally exhausted; his mind hadn't shut down from the day before.

> **Kyle should never have been thrown into the potential lion's den of virtual piranhas without training to learn critical skills imperative for managing virtual groups.**

For virtual managers like Kyle, 5:00 PM doesn't mean the day is over. After dinner, he heads to his den and holds a teleconference with Quality Assurance and an upset customer in Singapore.

Will this damn day ever end?

Today's work world is different. Workers are different. Employers are different. And expectations are different for leadership, management, employees, and customers. The globalization of employment and corporate outreach has morphed beyond what many futurists even imagined.

- Take Google: As the Emerald City of the virtual world, it feeds into every crevice and cranny of the internet. With over 70 brick and mortar offices in 50 plus countries and 88,000 full-time employees, at any one time thousands of virtual job openings appear on different job boards at Google.

- On Facebook, it's not uncommon to discover that over 10,000 jobs—all virtual—are available.

- Companies like Apple offer an "at-home advisor" position that is entirely virtual—employees from their "place of choice" as customer service reps.

- Xerox reveals that it has over 8,000 home-based employees in its virtual workplace programs. And Dell offers options: Do you want to work in its office or from your home?

- Insurance giant United Healthcare employees over 55,000 individuals virtually.

Have I got your attention?

Today's workplace is different and it requires vastly different leadership skills than those used in the traditional organization. If you are like Kyle, wouldn't you like to know the leadership skills and training that are needed for the virtual world that is required for any manager to operate effectively in the expanding business world? It's essential training that any leader working a remote team should have received from the get-go.

With the advent of the "virtual workplace," and the drive for team-based organizations, it is critical that professional managers understand two elements:

1. How modern technology has caused a change in the manner of group dynamics.

2. How team members need to be managed.

Kyle should never have been thrown into the potential lion's den of virtual piranhas without training to learn critical skills imperative for managing virtual groups. One of the most common mistakes is the assumption that if one is a good team manager in a face-to-face scenario, he or she will excel in a virtual one. In fact, the opposite is usually true: This person will fail.

Combining technology and group dynamics with a working knowledge of how group motivation works and the different technological tools available will lay the groundwork for the team leader to guide the newly developed virtual teams to their full potential.

Yes, Kyle is overwhelmed and it's no wonder. The workplace and the communications he is dealing with are nothing like what his MBA explored just five years ago. He asks himself and others in his position: *Will virtual leadership methods have to change to manage our remote teams?*

Ron's Takeaway

There is a "difference" between face-to-face management, and virtual leadership. While some of the elements may be the same, the emphasis of communication, trust, and utilization of technology will vary and has a stronger influence than what is used in face-to-face interactions. It's the virtual divide.

The virtual world is present and growing. All businesses, regardless of size, need to be mindful of the challenges, issues around conflicts. including awareness and recognition of its existence and resolution plus the opportunities.

Trends in Global Virtual Teams

The biggest challenges for global virtual teams:

- Colleagues who do not participate (79%)
- Pace of decision making (79%) influence
- Time required to make decisions (75%)
- Different role expectations held by team members (74%)
- Follow-through of team members (74%)

The greatest issues impacting productivity:

- Understanding the full context of what people communicate (51%)
- Managing conflict (48%)
- Establishing trust and building relationships (45%)
- Only 34% have had formal global leadership training

Source: RW3 CultureWizard www.rw-3.com (with permission)

CHAPTER 2

TEAM ROLES

Let's face it, managing is just hard work.

I have a question for you: Do you watch football? Is the best position as the quarterback or the tackle?

If you are a football fan like I am, you know that a winning coach matches each player's skills to the best position for him on the team. The ongoing challenge every coach faces is to determine how to put the best players in the right positions to create the best chance of winning the game.

Obviously, someone who has the power and size of the tackle would not be suited as a running back. How long would a kicker stay in one piece if he had to fill in as a guard? Football, as other professional team sports do, understands that one position is not more valuable than the other—each player has skills that are best suited for specific roles.

It's no different when it comes to virtual teams. The challenge is to have each person working in a role in which the team has the best chances of success. For Kyle, his challenge is how to find out which role is best suited for each person on his team.

Let's say that Kyle has put together a great team of people from all around the country. But he needs more. To create the Super Bowl of teams, he begins his quest to learn who is on the Super Bowl of Virtual Teams.

The pioneer of the Team Role theory, Dr. Meredith Belbin, defines team roles as "a tendency to behave, contribute, and interact with others in specific ways." But we are not talking about finding what our personalities are, in the way a Myers-Briggs assessment would do. As team leaders, you have to handle conflicts, differing attitudes, and personal relationships. Let's face it, managing is just hard work. Period. Ongoing research shows that only one person in ten has the natural leadership abilities that are needed. This means that managers and leaders must take the time to learn the different methods: What works best for you as a leader?

> In Europe and Asia, Belbin Team Roles have been the method of choice for over 25 years.

The beauty of Team Roles is that it provides a common language that everyone on a team can understand. In the United States, most team leaders are aware of assessments, such as Myers-Briggs and DiSC. In Europe and Asia, Belbin Team Roles have been the method of choice for over 25 years. I consider the Team Roles as being the best kept secret in the United States but they are gaining acceptance. What U.S. organizations use Belbin's concept? They are household names like:

- Best Buy

- PepsiCo

- United Nations

- The United States Marines

- Siemens

- Staples

- Xerox

- Wells Fargo

- BMW

- United States Nuclear Regulatory Commission

- Kaiser Permanente

What the Belbin Team Roles look at are different kinds of behavior and styles of interaction that you have with each other rather than personality traits. So why do you want to look at behavior?

- **It can change.** Personalities are set and not likely to change. It's essential to look at what changes may be necessary in your behavior as well as the rest of the team. Use a positive feedback on behavior. There are four actions to assist in personal development that I deem essential. They are listed in Chapter 3.

- **It is something that you can actually see.** Behavior and mannerisms are visible. You need to understand that what you actually do affects those around you just as a team member's behavior will affect others on the team, including you. By giving and receiving feedback on how a team member acts, you guide the ability to agree or disagree with one another.

- **You can change based on a situation.** Think about how your behavior can be reinforced by a kind word regarding what you are best suited to do or are best at. My wife can tell you that I am totally different working at home than I am in the office. My personality is still the same but my office behavior is different.

- **It is understandable.** Belbin Team Roles identify an individual's strengths and how each individual will fit into the team. Part of the concept is that everybody fits into a box—just not the same box. It is a fantastic way to help a person to realize his or her individual strengths and contribute to the team by doing something that he or she is good at and enjoys doing.

- **You are predictable.** Since behavior can be seen, it can be predicted. People may not always act as you expected them to act—after all we are humans. Yet, often one settles into ways of working and talking with others the same way over a period of time.

Meet the Roles

There are nine different Team Roles that a person will fall into and each one has a different way of contributing to a team's success.

1. People-based roles

- *Resource Investigator:* Strengths include being extroverted, enthusiastic, communicative, explores opportunities, and develops contacts. Weaknesses include being overly-optimistic, losing interest, and burning out.

- *The Team-worker:* Strengths are cooperative, mild, perceptive, diplomatic, listens, builds, averts friction, and calms the waters. Weaknesses include being indecisive and stepping back when pressed for a decision.

- *The Coordinator:* Strengths include being mature, confident, a good chairperson, clarifies goals, promotes decision making, and delegates well. Weaknesses include possible over-delegation and may rub people the wrong way by how work is allocated.

2. Thought-based roles

- *The Plant:* Strengths include being creative, imaginative, unorthodox, solves difficult problems. Weaknesses are being introverted; not the best communicator; and may be absent-minded.

- *The Monitor Evaluator:* Strengths include being focused, strategic and discerning; sees all options; and judges accurately. Weaknesses include being overly critical of the team, and sometimes struggles to inspire others.

- *The Specialist:* Strengths include being highly focused, self-starting, dedicated, and provides knowledge and skills. Weaknesses include getting bogged down with details; possibly losing sight of objectives due to paying attention to the tiniest details; or deciding to do the task to just get it done.

3. Action-based roles

- *An Implementer:* Strengths include being disciplined, reliable, conservative, efficient, and able to turn ideas into practical actions. Weaknesses include reluctance to change or inflexible if things do change.

- *The Completer:* Strengths include being disciplined, reliable, conservative, efficient, and can turn actions into completed projects. Weaknesses include worrying unnecessarily, perfection driven, and unwilling to delegate.

- *The Shaper:* Strengths include being challenging, dynamic, thriving on pressure, and having the drive and courage to overcome obstacles. Weaknesses include being over-enthusiastic, possibly argumentative, and having a more aggressive approach.

The good news is that there are some free versions of the Belbin available on the web. The better news is to actually take the Belbin Team Role assessment from someone, like myself, who is certified as a Belbin trainer and has access to the extensive Belbin database to determine the individual strengths of each team member. Not only does it measure each team member who takes a very quick online assessment, but also at least four people who you have worked with for at least six months to gain their perspective on how they see you.

Think about when you go to the bookstore and you look at an astrology book. Have you looked at it and said, "This sounds just like me—how did the author know everything about me?" He or she didn't. Whatever was written was done in generalities.

Unfortunately, how you see yourself may not be the same as how you are seen by those you work with. To create the ultimate team-working experience and outcome, it's recommended that you combine your assessment with other observers. The result? A more accurate evaluation and result. And, if you are in a company that uses Lean Six Sigma, Belbin has a team report that can align Team Roles with that program.

Do you prime the pump?

In my office sits an old cast iron water pump. It has been a constant point of reflection for me for the last 30 years. It is there to remind me of my early years. There is an old Zig Ziglar story about how the water pump needs to be primed to get to the good cold water. I use that same concept in communications by having one-on-one meetings every Monday with each of my team members to prime the communications pump.

Is "work" the reason I communicate with them. Well, yes … and no. We don't talk about "work"; we talk about personal things. It's about being connected and caring about those on my team. If anything about work surfaces, it's very little and not sought. After all, we have work reviews during a brief weekly status meeting that I call my *Stand-up Meeting* (I call it this because meetings go quickly if people have to stand and I reduced an hour meeting to under 15 minutes) This one-on-one meeting is to develop that personal bond and it has a huge impact on the level of trust between us.

> **The lack of face-to-face communications is one of the largest obstacles to circumvent.**

How many of you only hear from your boss when something has gone wrong or is needed? How many of you have heard from a boss just to see how you are doing; to congratulate you on a family celebration; or even wish you happy birthday or thanking you, telling you that you are a valuable part of the company? Communicating with your team doesn't always have to be about "work."

Teams need the ability to see each other and develop a bond.

Research demonstrates that the lack of face-to-face communications is one of the largest obstacles to circumvent. This can only be countered by understanding the new communications technology and how to use it. The virtual organization is relatively new but there are many tools for the virtual leader to use, and many are free.

Understanding the relationships and values of each is critical to the ability of a company to survive in the world market today. The introduction of new communication technologies develops opportunities and expands change in the organization itself (e.g., virtual teams, virtual organizations).

Technology and leadership are becoming the two sides of the business coin. There are many positive corporate reasons to encourage the development of a strong technology-based virtual organizational system: communicating; traveling expenses and delays; weather worries; and logistical nightmares are all reduced or eliminated.

Teams need the ability to see each other face-to-face and have time to develop a bond. The virtual team can also accomplish this by combining individual photos and creating a team photograph.

Develop and post it on the team website and/or on the portal that team members communicate through. Since the team cannot meet at the water cooler for informal swapping of stories, the team leader can create a "virtual water cooler," a digital space for them to talk about feelings about what is either happening or just as a catch up about the latest movie or activity the team member experienced.

Research has identified the range of communications from email, teleconferencing, computer video conferencing, and face-to-face meetings. Email was the lowest unsocial presence in that it lacks the physical presence and the ability to see the nonverbal body language that is the foundation of the "rich" information achieved with face-to-face communications. It is the mutual eye gaze, nods that help to reduce disruptions in communications that set the feelings of personalization and understanding the messages being sent. Contrary to the belief of many, this can easily be done within the virtual world.

Virtual Tools Are a Click Away

Free video conferencing tools available to you include:

- **www.Zoom.us** – easy to use and allows for the use of video conference rooms. They have a free version that lets you host up to 100 participants with a 40- minute time limit. Great quality of video and I use it as my primary video tool.

- **www.Slack.com** – has a free plan and can select different channels (blogs, events, products, etc.) and individual team members can have group chats and share files.

- **www.flock.com** – free version has 5GB file storage for your team. Search up to 10K messages. Video up to four users and screen sharing.

Free or Low-Cost Project Management Tools:

- **www.Asana.com** – has a free version project dashboard for up to 15 team members and has unlimited tasks, projects, and conversations.

- **Google Drive** – delivering 100 GB of memory for $1.99/ month, it can make changes in real time and is easy to use. Starts with 15 GB free storage.

- **www.Dashlane.com** – a password manager that provides access without actually trying to remember which team member has what password. Even has a password generator. Free version has unlimited password and data storage, security monitoring service and breach alert.

- **www.LastPass.com** – allows for you to share access to files without having the actual password. Some may need access to secured folders, websites, PayPal, click bank, lead pages, etc. You can give login access with folders and can remove access as needed.

Ron's Takeaway

Virtual management is not totally accepted by managers. They argue that the value of the face-to-face interaction will be lost because they will be less likely to experience a sense of social interaction within the group. While the concerns are real and need to be considered by the virtual leader, good planning and a well thought-out program can overcome them.

The team needs to have at least one video conference a week so there is an opportunity to connect socially before a work meeting starts. Discourage the "art of multi-tasking"—it will shorten meeting time—something everyone will support.

When savvy managers discover the power of the Belbin tool, they set the stage for working at a job and in an environment that they actually enjoy. Below are a variety of sites to explore.

Belbin Sources

Belbin (Worldwide headcounters)	Belbin.com
Belbin USA/North America	Belbin.ImprovingTeams.com

International Belbin Sources

Belbin Australia	Belbin.com.au
Belbin Chile	MomentumConsultores.cl
Belbin China	Belbin-China.com
Belbin Colombia	PSAConsultores.com
Belbin Costa Rica	Conexosoluciones.net/inicio
Belbin Czech Republic	Belbin.cz
England	Belbin.com

Virtual Nuggets

CHAPTER 3

IMPACT OF CULTURAL DIFFERENCES ON VIRTUAL TEAMS

*The most productive leadership team in the multinational firm
will have an equal balance of different management styles.*

E ndo was thinking as fast as he could. I was his counterpart in America; he was a native of Japan. I felt like I was talking in my normal speed and rhythm but realized that it was full throttle for him. And I had assumed that he was hearing me as my colleagues in America did. I was wrong. Endo was listening … then translating what I said into Japanese … then responding back to me in English. My normal flow of speaking was way too fast; I didn't pause so he could absorb and digest what I was saying.

It's surprising to me that Endo didn't throw me under the bus. Although I didn't know that it was a struggle for him when we communicated remotely. That turned around when we had a face-to-face over sake one evening when I visited him on his turf. "You speak too swiftly; you don't give me enough time to process an opinion and give you an answer. By then you are already talking about something else."

Coming from a culture where personal relationships are imperative, Endo was concerned that if he had spoken up, he would have offended me. Several sakes later, I vowed to myself to slow down and remember that even though Endo spoke excellent English, he still was Japanese and processed in his language before he responded to me in mine.

Endo and all peoples where English isn't their first language need to process what they HEAR you say and what they THINK you mean in their language BEFORE they will respond back in English. It's a challenge. Additionally, you always need to be aware that your meaning can be lost in translation. Word your conversations simply—don't embellish.

Leading a virtual team requires skills that go beyond those used with traditional project management. To support these skills, there are four positive actions that you as a leader can implement.

They are to:

1. Establish regular face-to-face meetings. When teams see each other, they develop stronger bonds.

2. Create a team collage photograph and post it on a graphic folder on the team website.

3. Swap stories around a virtual water cooler. Share stories, events, activities that will or have happened … just like you would do if you were all under one roof. Your virtual water cooler can be a digital space for them to talk about feelings regarding what is either happening or not.

4. Include at least one video conferencing stand-up meeting each week.

The workplace delivers a range of communications from email, teleconferencing, computer video conferencing, and face-to-face meetings. There are times when one form of communicating will outshine another.

Email has the lowest unsocial presence.

- *Emailing* has the lowest unsocial presence outside of noncommunicating. It lacks the physical presence and the ability to see the nonverbal body language that is the foundation of the "rich" information achieved with face-to-face communications.

- *Teleconferencing* doesn't generate the pluse of a face-to-face, but it does carry a "voice" and with that voice, tones. You can hear pleasure and joy in a tone; disapproval; confusion; and the ability to sense hurt feelings.

- *Computer Video Conferencing* works when all parties are on the same broadband, and the power supply is a constant —different speeds can create a visual distraction as well as voice distortion.

- *Face-to-Face Meetings* … meaning in person (skype) … puts it all in a physical presence. It is the mutual eye gazing and nodding that help to reduce disruptions in communications and to set the feelings of personalization and understanding that the messages are being received.

Teams will combine all of them. Of course, some will be used more than others.

As a leader, you may need to experiment and determine which method works best. The time of year as well as the time of the day will also factor in. If there are unusual occurances happening in a team member's environment (politically, environmentally, or personally), the leader needs to be cognizant of this.

In many multinational companies, the team building occurs without major problems. In others, teamwork is marked by frustrations, unresolved conflict, hidden agendas, unspoken questions, and confusion about decisions and goals. In reality, the most productive leadership team in the multinational firm will have an equal balance of different management styles.

The virtual organization challenges many of the leadership models that have been so successful in the past. The new leadership model demands that the virtual leader become situational: a combination of the transactional, transformational, and servant.

The reason is that most are based on one-on-one relationships and communication skills. Technology has complicated the mix. It is already becoming apparent that face-to-face teams are using more and more of the communication tools that are used by the virtual teams.

Different cultures respond to different styles of leadership.

When it comes to virtual teams, a climate of knowledge and mutual respect is essential in understanding who each member is, including what his or her cultural influences are. When you do, you propel the success of your team and increase its productivity. Improvements will continue in global communication and the increase of virtual teams into working relationships with other cultures.

The virtual leader's managerial experiences along with the length of time a team member has been with a company and organizational factors have a significant relationship with leadership style. When teams become sensitive to their own leadership needs, then they will be more likely to understand those same needs of other cultures and their own team members. The savvy team leader will understand that different cultures respond to different styles of leadership. There is no right way.

For instance, the consultative style is task-oriented and focuses on the end result. It is the most common leadership style in a multicultural non-Western setting but may indicate that the decision-making process is lengthy and subject to delays.

Mutually establishing and reviewing with your team what the expectations are will motivate them toward completion of the overall objectives. This will be a major endeavor for the leader on all of the different shores.

Ron's Takeaway

In North America, leaders must learn more of the global cultural differences in management styles. The same goes for those who come from other countries. The result: The blend of the different cultures can produce a powerful virtual team if given the opportunity.

Remote leaders need to keep up-to-date. Some of my favorite blogs and articles I follow and turn to include the sites below.

Multicultural Virtual Teams

Managing cross-functional and virtual teams
https://bit.ly/2PKKd7d

Challenges in and Strategies for Working with Multicultural Virtual Teams
https://bit.ly/2oeBxcT

Managing Cultural Diversity for a Virtual Workforce
https://bit.ly/2odBVYW

Managing Cultural Distance in Virtual Teams
https://bit.ly/2MBvRs6

Managing Cross Cultural Remote Teams
https://bit.ly/2KcypvD

CHAPTER 4

TECHNOLOGY AND VIRTUAL LEADERSHIP

With the technology, it is essential to understand the differences in communication issues, styles, and strategies.

Norman, Oklahoma – United States of America, 1986. You could call me ignorant when it came to technology—any type of technology. If I was in the office early, I would wait for someone to come in who knew how to turn on the machine to make a pot of coffee. Then I got a cup. If the copy machine decided not to copy, I begged for help. When I saw men (and it was always men) in the airport holding what looked like bricks to their ears that turned out to be the first generation of a mobile phone, I said, "Not me!" When computers came into the office, it was my secretary that turned mine on. I was a clueless manager in the late 1980s—a living, breathing dinosaur.

The "change" happened when my secretary was no longer my secretary. I was totally lost … and it was obvious that if I was going to continue in my position as the group manager of a high technology company, I better get found.

And found I did. It started with the flip phone … now a relic; it was a marvel to me. And yes, I dug in my heels when it was time to transition to a smart phone. I now use multiple laptops and know more software and programs than I could have ever imagined.

When it was time to push myself further, who would have thought that I would earn both my master's and doctorate online? Not me … and certainly not "the me" of the '80s or even the '90s. Yet now I work with teams all over the world, even from a cruise ship.

Today's managers are not only extremely comfortable with the daily use of computers, they now also demand that whatever equipment they use, it must be more flexible and easy to use. With the technology, it is essential to understand the differences in communication issues, styles, and strategies. One of the downfalls of technology, and the overuse of it, is the easily missed personal interaction, which include the little visual expressions that communicate ideas or opinions. You don't see them in emails, text messages, or teleconferences. Facial expressions and physical gestures do not exist in the virtual world.

Technology must compensate for it. This can be done using technology where all team members can participate and be contributing with their knowledge and opinions on a real-time basis.

In face-to-face conversation, we can see if listeners are confused, frown, smile, nod their heads or look like they are paying attention. All of these cues are trouble flags that tell you that the listener did not understand your message, is puzzled, or is just not paying attention.

Did you know that only a fraction of the full meaning of your communication is contained in the words you use? That would mean that reading (email) could therefore convey only a small portion of the meaning of what you are trying to communicate.

In 1999, the first emoji was created in Japan to add "emotion" to electronic communications.

If you've ever been around teens, you've heard the dreaded "teen tone," the one that clearly implies that you are a loser, stupid, or a moron. Tones can also relay excitement, happiness (and unhappiness), or a question.

In the real world, your actual words combined with the tones that are attached to them make up roughly half of the communication circle. The remainder comes from "body language"— the physiology that can be attached to spoken words as well as unspoken ones. The well-known saying makes the point: A picture is worth a thousand words.

Unless there are images attached to emails, texts, faxes and phone calls, your point may have been missed if you rely exclusively on electronic communications. The electronic tribe took notice. In 1999, the first emoji was created in Japan to add "emotion" to electronic communications via nonverbal cues. Hello happy faces, angry faces and everything else in-between.

There are other differences that a manager needs to be aware of when planning the use of technical tools. Social cues are essential to understand and be aware of. The heavy use of the virtual communication tools has been found to increase negative communication tones that have included assertive and hostile language and an increased sense of depersonalization. Teams become even more remote. A team that has a one-hour time zone difference can act like there is a fourteen-hour one. Additional management attention may be required to establish better collaboration and coordination mechanisms.

With teams that start out remotely, physical meetings may never occur.

When a company is diversified in physical locations or if it has a single location with team members scattered across time zones and sometimes countries, the virtual team's ability to keep up with technological developments is a major factor in a company remaining competitive in a rapidly changing environment. Is there resistance to virtual teams? Yes, they are not openly accepted by all business communities. Yet, the tools that make working virtual successful are also heavily used by all work teams.

AT&T created the 50 Yard Rule: When communications exceed 50 yards, the effectiveness of the communications is greatly diminished. Its research found that the use of voice communications was placed second, with face-to-face meetings being first.

Within companies that have advanced technology, it has become more difficult to draw a distinction between conventional face-to-face teams and virtual teams due to the nature of technology used by these modern organizations.

This is a critical point. Managers must keep in mind that for the virtual team to reach its full potential, face-to-face meetings up front lay the groundwork for the use of the various technology sources as the project continues. With the initial "live" connection the team was formed, which was ideal. With teams that start out remotely, physical meetings may never occur. The savvy team leader knows that he or she needs to put extra emphasis on the team dynamics and interaction so that "remote" does not feel remote.

Right now, advances in technology are outpacing the ability of many companies to apply it because they do not have the infrastructure or processes to integrate them. Leaders find themselves playing catch up to learn the tools and how to integrate them into their existing culture and business processes. In terms of e-leadership, this survey showed that foundational skills traditionally associated with leadership, such as having the communication skills required to unify and motivate others toward common goals, are as important as ever.

An email is a popular means of digital communications in Western countries. There are exceptions in East Asia such as Japan and Korea where it is a choice for communications among themselves and within their organizations. When they work outside their own environment, they prefer face-to-face. In addition, in those countries, seniority in the rank requires the use of special codes of conduct to show respect for executives at the senior level. This aspect of the cultural difference discourages the use of email for communications from lower ranking employees with the senior management while it accepts it as effective among peers.

Westerners should understand that their method to create and maintain direct eye contact is inappropriate in Eastern countries.

Due to these basic beliefs founded on Confucian teachings, the use of the digital conference call or video conferencing would be appropriate. In Ireland, the opposite is true. Due to the different quality levels of internet access, the use of video conferencing is very poor, so email is the communication tool of choice.

Ron's Takeaway

Effective managers need to understand three essentials. They must have a basic understanding of the different communications technology available today. They must know how it could be used in their environment. And they must know what cultural preferences and restrictions will influence the use by the team members and their countries.

There are a variety of free resources for any leader and team to use for audio communication. Below are a few of my favorites.

Join.me   Join.me   Free one on one and instant meeting

FreeConference   FreeConferenceCall.com   5 online video participants (400 audio participants)

Jitsi   Jitsi.org   Open sourced, free, share desktop, invite users, edit documents together

ezTalks   ezTalks.com   Free for up to 100 participants, screen sharingand record

CHAPTER 5

THERE IS NO PERFECT LEADERSHIP STYLE

*The virtual leader must provide results
for the company by taking care of its employees.*

Yes, you read correctly: There is no perfect leadership style. I read a lot. Years ago, I remember reading a leadership book that told me if I was not a specific type of leader, I was a failure. Now that I am more experienced and wiser due to the lessons in life, as my Irish grandfather would say, that concept is pure blarney. Yet, you can't pick up a leadership book today that doesn't shout out: This is the only way to truly lead a team, a group, or an organization. My grandfather was right: It's pure blarney.

First and foremost, the virtual leader has a huge responsibility to achieve results in an environment that demands balancing methods to accomplish the goals of the team. And, the virtual leader must provide results for the company by taking care of its employees. How do you do that? Simply this: You take care of the employees by getting the results needed by the company. Both you and the employees have to win or you did not do your job.

The nail that sticks up gets hit the most.

You can fill an entire library with books telling you what the role of a leader is, but the virtual leader has two roles in an organization:

1. to simulate creativity by innovation; and

2. to urge participation to make achievements.

Which role is the best? That's a good question. A virtual leader is more likely to be someone who takes a stand on a creative position, empowers other people to be part of that vision, and has the faith to make it happen simply because it feels like it is the right thing to do. It is by stamina alone that it is carried to fulfillment. In truth, care must be taken.

At times, every manager needs to step up to the plate and be a leader.

In Japan, there is a wise saying: The nail that sticks up gets hit the most.

Some feel that leaders are people who *do the right things* and managers are people who *do things right*. Another way of saying it is that managers get other people to *do a job*, while leaders get it done by getting people *to want to do it*.

Leaders are interested in providing direction, vision, goals, objectives, intention, purpose, and effectiveness. Definitely, the right things to focus on. Managers are more interested in efficiency, the how-to of the day-to-day, and the short run of doing things right.

Is it that simplified? That easy? I wish, but it isn't—you have to be able to fit into both roles as the situations change. I love being in the leadership mode myself but there are times in which there has to be results. Those "sometimes" bring out the manager in me. When I was the Director of U.S. Manufacturing for LSI/Engino Logic in Wichita, Kansas, I would send out an email just before the last two weeks of the quarter telling employees that we would "be friends" next month. That meant how I would be deeply involved with making sure the products were shipped and customers were happy. The cost of failure could mean jobs. Lost jobs were something I would not accept for my employees.

At times, every leader needs to switch positions and be a manager.

In seven years at LSI, we never missed a revenue target. The power of seeing the factory and virtual teams pulling in the same direction is an experience to see in action.

Every manager should have the knowledge to set the goals needed to be successful. Yet, it is the leader who accomplishes those goals by working with his or her people to make them happen. Is one better than the other? Heck no. It is not that one is better than the other. Every company needs both to be successful. At times, every manager needs to step up to the plate and be a leader. And, at times, every leader needs to switch positions and be a manager.

To be a successful virtual leader, you must deliver on commitments by having the support of others. Lone heroes who transformed organizations single-handedly have long ago been dispelled as myths. Today's successful virtual leader recognizes the importance of relationships in achieving success in our fast moving and ever-changing landscape.

Virtual Teams Are Different

Because virtual teams are different, they need to be led and managed differently. If a leader was to display typical corporate leadership traits, the team would most likely underperform. I've found that my leadership style has changed, evolved, and transitioned. It has become a combination of styles. Leadership is not a one size fits all; it needs to be tuned into the needs of each group that a leader heads up.

Meet the Transformational Leader

The transformational style of leadership is one of the most popular and focuses on humanistic rather than the authoritative, top-down, transactional style. It is founded on the belief that inner development is the first step to outward leadership action.

At the heart of the transformational style is a very specific skill set that is different than other methods. The use of charisma is a bridging method. Charismatic leaders can get people to move beyond their own wants to a level that they willfully strive for the benefit of the business unit. This focus on charisma suggests that effective leaders should be proactive, change oriented, innovative, motivating and inspiring, and have a vision or mission with which they infuse the group. Employees will respond with a stronger commitment to the team and are willing to give that extra effort when the demand is there.

Multiple research has demonstrated how transformational leadership creates a positive relationship between management and the workforce in such a way that it functions with improved performance.

The Type of Leader That Works the Best for My Teams

There are many styles of leadership but the one that works best in my virtual organization is identified as servant-leadership. The primary goal of servant-leadership is that a leader's first responsibility is to serve those within their virtual team. For example, Stephen Covey said, "The servant-leadership concept is a principle, a natural law, and getting our social value systems and personal habits aligned with this ennobling principle is one of the great challenges of our lives."

Here's where the difference lies from the more standard types of leadership models. Traditional leaders practice a top-down or "top of the pyramid" approach—it's about the ability to exercise power over others. Those who practice servant leadership are not into exercising over others; they are into sharing power. Plus, the "needs" of others are at the forefront coupled with helping develop and perform as highly as possible. For me, the fundamental motivation for leadership should be a desire to serve my people by taking care of them. Servant-leadership is not about lack of direction but about implementation. Servant-leaders seek to enhance the personal as well as professional development of their team members.

Some think that leading a virtual team is easier and less demanding than leading a traditional brick and mortar operation. Not so. As a leader of a virtual team, you must be in tune with your individual team members as well as the group as a whole.

Servant Leadership Attributes

The servant-leader is different from other forms of leadership in that service is at its core and has a moral imperative. The leader who does choose a service role sets about providing the resources of information, time, attention, material and other resources that each team member needs to achieve success.

Larry Spears is the former executive director of the Spears Center for Servant Leadership. He has been a great friend in allowing me to share his 10 critical characteristics of the servant-leader with you:

1. **Listening:** Servant-leaders must reinforce these important skills by making a deep commitment to listening intently to others.

2. **Empathy:** The most successful servant-leaders are those who have become skilled empathetic listeners.

3. **Healing:** In *The Servant as Leader*, Greenleaf writes: "There is something subtle communicated to one who is being served and led if, implicit in the compact between servant-leader and led is the understanding that the search for wholeness is something they share."

4. **Awareness:** General awareness and especially self-awareness strengthens the servant-leader.

5. **Persuasion:** Reliance upon persuasion, rather than positional authority.

6. **Conceptualization:** To be a servant-leader, thinking must be stretched to encompass broader-based conceptual

thinking. There is a delicate balance between conceptualization and day-to-day focus.

7. **Foresight:** The ability to foresee the outcome of a situation is hard to define, but easy to identify. It is deeply rooted within the intuitive mind. Foresight is the one servant-leader characteristic with which one may be born and is the central ethic of leadership.

8. **Stewardship:** Holding something in trust for another.

9. **Commitment to the growth of people:** Belief that people have an intrinsic value beyond their tangible contributions as workers.

10. **Building community:** Servant-leaders seek to identify a means for building community among those who work within a given institution.

Creative Problem Solving

Without an understanding of the conditions of creativity, brainstorming, questioning, mind maps, association, analogy, fantasy, relaxation, role-play, or quantum leap thinking, a problem solver will wind up short of reaching a goal. It will be compounded even more as team activity, which have a number of components, is utilized as a tool for creative thinking. These components include:

- separation and organization of tasks

- synergistic interaction that comes from the give and take of individual ideas

- mutual encouragement that comes from common goals and healthy competition

- team concept, i.e. a team can accomplish goals and generate more ideas than isolated individuals

Of the four, team concept is the largest. In creative problem solving, there are key impediments that are demonstrated by impaired problem solvers. There are inhibiting beliefs, go nowhere questions, impaired instruments, and ignorance of problem-solving techniques. The savvy leader needs to be on alert and seek to resolve them as quickly as possible.

Can creativity be shut down? Absolutely. Certain beliefs tend to shut down a person's creativity, but also for the team as well. One of my favorite quotes is by Donald Noone, "The most underutilized resource in most companies is the creative power of its employees."

There are seven different types of persons whom I call *creativity zappers*. They are individuals that you as a virtual leader will have to contend with. Expect to see some (if not all) of them in your career:

1. *Ringleaders* - believe that they are surrounded by idiots, or folks who are not blessed with their wisdom;

2. *Complainers* - embrace the irrational;

3. *Sufferers* - all problems, large or small, are troublesome;

4. *Purists* - the solution must be perfect—they don't feel that any solutions are good enough;

5. *Undecided* - committed to waiting—minimum speed, even a few steps backward, are just fine;

6. *Pretenders* - these are the people pleasers; they never come up with their own solutions to problems; and

7. *Ordinary* - hate change, like a routine and predictability.

Enhance Creativity and Collaboration in Your Teams

The group creative process is beginning to receive higher attention among the executive ranks. There are as many tips on generating group creativity as there are consultants.

Everyone has his or her own slant on methods but one of the most functional were the six tips I created.

1. Healthy relationships are at the heart of collaboration.
Get the team to connect at the personal as well as professional level, but as people, to build trust and that personal bond needed to support each other. The easiest way to do this in a virtual environment is by using video conferencing and get together at least once a year for a face-to-face meeting.

2. Connect the project with big picture company objectives.
Explain the role of the team so that everyone understands how important they are for the company to meet the corporate goals. I like to show how the team will impact the end customers and help improve their lives.

3. Create an atmosphere of safety, trust, and respect.
Encourage differences of opinions and views. This is needed to get past that fear factor of being afraid of what others will think.

4. Make your ideas visible and tangible.

Use drawings, charts, tables, etc. Working for the Japanese showed me the power of that visual reinforcement.

5. Use positive leadership.

Our job is to remove the barriers and provide the needed resources. Don't be that tyrant or negative boss. Be proactive by building those team connections across the organization. Give credit where credit is due and recognize team performance as well as individuals.

6. Add fun factors.

Above all, have fun.

Creating new ideas and seeing them come to life should be an event that is positive—even those that don't work out.

Ron's Takeaway

The virtual manager of the 21st century has to continually find more innovative ways to involve employees in idea generation. To be competitive, every company needs to get extraordinary performance from ordinary employees. It has become more important than ever to be creative, in tapping the potential energy of employees from all levels of the organization.

Articles to add to your tool box for a variety of Leadership Styles include six that you should become familiar with and use interchangeably.

Leadership Styles

The pacesetting leader is the type of leader who expects the group to be one that is already high performing, motivated, and skilled at getting things done.   https://bit.ly/2wlXYBh

The authoritative leader inspires the group to follow his lead to a new vision or mission. An authoritative leader is good at getting people to see how their work fits into the company's goals.

https://bit.ly/2NpXf8M

The affiliative leader can create that emotional bond that gets people to feel part of the larger organization. The affiliative leader loves working in a stressful environment because he or she thrives on receiving praise and being the center of attention.   https://bit.ly/2PGn2v3

The coaching leader has a passion for helping people develop their personal strengths and be successful.   https://bit.ly/2MUBQYq

The coercive leader demands that his or her directions be followed without question during an emergency.   https://bit.ly/2LyldvM

The democratic leader is the consensus builder and encourages not only participation but ownership of the ideas.   https://bit.ly/2PHFkvP

CHAPTER 6

Do You Have What It Takes to Be a Great Virtual Leader?

*The virtual leader is significantly
different from a virtual manager.*

Every leader has a problem child. I dreaded the day a new professor landed under my umbrella. She'd been with the university for years, yet we had never met face-to-face.

She had moved to Florida from the West Coast, so our first meeting was via video. Obviously, a mistake had been made. The person on my monitor wasn't the person who was in the file I had reviewed before our virtual meeting. The person I was talking to was outgoing, energetic, enthusiastic, and positive— all traits that I look for in my team members.

When she moved to Florida, she made some decisions. Health wise, she had lost 100 pounds. No wonder she didn't look like the photo I saw. She also made some decisions that she was indeed competent, contrary to what others thought. She had recharged her life.

Over the last four decades, I have worked hard to understand what makes a proactive servant-leader. What I have used with my teams was not learned in the six years I was in the Marines. Oh, I got basic skills—the authoritative style. Quickly, I saw that it wasn't the ideal model when I transitioned to the corporate side. My leadership style needed refining and defining. What evolved came from my time with Western Digital, Hitachi, LSI Logic, and Ashford University. I had multiple occasions to learn from great leaders (and even experience some bad ones).

My leadership style needed refining and defining.

With the years of seeing the very best and worst examples of leadership, I have concluded that there are really five basic competencies to be an effective virtual leader: the *facilitator, barrier buster, coach,* and *lead by example,* and be an *inspirational leader.* I am not saying that there are no others, but I would put these five at the top of any list. Few have all five competencies—General Colin Powell is one of those exceptions.

Facilitator: Knows how to find the resources needed to get any job done. This goes beyond just getting the job assignment but helps provide tools to get it done properly. The resources could be:

- financial funds;
- additional people to help;
- training (a recent survey shows only 22% received training to increase productivity in virtual teams); and
- guidance on how to hold a virtual meeting.

Barrier buster: Knows how to create breakthroughs. A barrier buster has the ability to rejuvenate the team by showing that the impossible is possible—that the wall that is perceived is merely a speed bump—a bump that can be easily gone over or around. As a barrier buster, your job is to be working to eliminate those policies, structures, and conflicts that get in the way of producing the best organizational results. Be willing to ask, "What can I do to help?" And then do it.

The virtual leader can really help with things like:

- interpersonal conflict;
- organizational silos;
- policies and procedures; and
- internal politics.

Coach: My favorite Japanese president at Hitachi was called *The Tornado*. He said,

> *Manage like you are the conductor of an orchestra. To make groups work, you recruit the best; provide the needed skills; guide them in working better together; and help them learn from their mistakes. The result is a group that works as one.*

Lead by example: *Do as I say … and as I do* is your motto when your style is leading by example. You need to set an example of how you want your team to be. Most have experienced a leader who says one thing but does another. In other words, he or she doesn't walk the talk. That is the same as hearing your parent say, "Do as I say, not as I do." The powerful thing to remember is that your people will be watching more of what you do than what you say you will do.

Do you:

- respond to emails or voice messages within 24 hours?

- provide the authority and resources to be successful?

- use face-to-face and video conferencing on a regular basis?

- share information and keep your people in the loop?

A recent study by CDN2 shows that 48% of virtual leaders have never met their virtual team members in person.

Inspirational leader: A leader needs to make sure that the goals and objectives are met—an inspiration creates a positive, results baring environment. Notice that I said leader; I did not refer to a manager. Both roles have a valuable place in an organization but the virtual leader is significantly different from a virtual manager. A virtual leader:

- *Motivates others to get past their own perceived barriers and to do their best work.*

  My Mondays start with one-on-one phone calls to make a personal connection by just saying hello and connecting on the personal side—what did they do for themselves, their families—there is no agenda. When my wife ran into a police car, you can be sure that my Monday call shared that with my team.

  My Thursdays include a video conference call with my team with an update from the side of the university I teach for. Then each person gives me a status on what he or she has been doing during the week as well as any issues that have surfaced. If appropriate, I, along with team members share thoughts.

> You are providing the knowledge that will be the foundation of each team member's career.

• *Provides the opportunities for a team member to work through tough problems and to make decisions based on his or her own beliefs.* The key is to work with the person on the problem but not be "the fixer." For anyone who is frustrated and stressed with the problem, you as the virtual leader have an excellent opportunity to use your experience as a teaching moment.

As the saying goes, "If you give a man a fish, you feed him for a day. If you teach him how to fish, you feed him for a lifetime." You are providing the knowledge that will be the foundation of each team member's career. Take the time to invest your most valuable asset: your time.

• *Pats them on the back when they make good decisions and provides guidance when they make the bad ones—and they will.* As a leader, it creates the opportunity to take the bad results to bond with your team members by providing mentoring support and guidance.

Ron's Takeaway

Regardless of what we are saying, your team is paying attention to what you do. If you want to make a change, have your people see you doing it. I would walk around the factory and move material carts into their taped sections on the factory floor (we had implanted visual management by taping areas for material placement). I reinforced the concept by doing and not just saying.

When you are on the phone or conference call with a team member, stop typing and pay attention. Think how frustrating it is when they can hear you typing on the keyboard and they know you are not totally tuned in to their problem. Or them.

Any manager can dictate an organization to be mediocre, but you will only get world class performance if you get your people to want it as much as you do. Be the motivator, the cheerleader and mentor.

Inspirational Leadership

It is not an easy thing to become that inspiring leader if you have not had a role model to help guide you. There are some very good articles that I have found to help me as I continually strive to improve myself. Take a minute and I believe that they may help give you some ideas.

1. How to Be an Inspiring Leader - *Harvard Business Review*
   https://bit.ly/2qbyBwm

2. 5 Keys to Inspiring Leadership, No Matter Your Style - *Entrepreneur*
   https://bit.ly/2ppsmqp

3. What Makes Leaders Inspirational to People? - *The Balance Careers*
   https://bit.ly/2pncftN

4. Why Great Leaders (Like Richard Branson) Inspire Instead of Motivate ...https://www.inc.com/marissa-levin/why-great-leaders-like-richard-branson-inspire-instead-of-motivate.html

CHAPTER 7

Are You a Manager or a Leader?

Leaders have two roles in a virtual organization,
to simulate creativity and innovation,
and to urge participation and achievement.

How many times have you said, or thought, if only I knew then what I know now? If you are like me, *plenty* would be your answer.

Kyle is no different. As a newbie manager, his frustration and stress levels were off the charts. He quickly discovered that his strategies and techniques from his face-to-face workplaces didn't work any longer. There was a reason why he was propelled into the remote leadership position. He was good. Too many times, individuals are placed into positions that they aren't trained for, just as Kyle was. He was good at what he did. But that was in the face-to-face workplace—a workplace that was 180 degrees from the remote workplace.

Stewing in his frustration guaranteed failure. He had to "get over it" to survive and succeed. He'd need to learn new ways, new methods, and new strategies of communication with his remote team. He had no other choice. Yes, Kyle had to really get over it. And he did.

According to The Maxwell Group, in a report released via its blog in 2018, new supervisors do not get leadership training until they've been in a leadership position for ten years. Not only is that an appalling revelation, but it means that if companies are operating under a type of unwritten training policy, they will fail, and fail quickly, with the expansion of the remote workplace.

The mystery of what leaders can and ought to do to spark the best performance from their people is an age-old question. While there are some, like management visionary Peter Drucker, who feel that management and leadership are part and parcel of the same job, there are many that feel that there is a distinct difference between the two.

I totally disagree, and you need to understand why.

Virtual Leaders

Leaders have two roles in a virtual organization, to simulate creativity and innovation, and to urge participation and achievement. Executives who are accustomed to having quantitative methods to assist their decision making have a more difficult time grasping the differences between management and leadership.

There is virtually no quantitative research that demonstrates which leadership behavior yields positive results.

In manufacturing operations, most senior management comes from the engineering or financial disciplines. That means that people in those positions are more comfortable with measurable results—anything in the "bean counting" arena appeals to them. In many business organizations, those who have excelled within sales or marketing look at the numbers and end results, forgetting that "training" is needed to get to the numbers desired. On the other hand, someone from human resources or an operations background would have a better understanding of the impact by qualitative means.

To date, there is virtually no quantitative research that demonstrates which leadership behavior yields positive results.

Which traits are the best for a virtual leader? It will more likely be someone who takes a stand on a creative position, empowers other people to be part of that vision, and has the faith to make it happen simply because he or she feels it is the right thing to do.

Some feel that leaders are people who do the right things and managers are people who do things right. Another way of saying it is that managers get other people to do a job, while leaders get it done by getting people to want to do it.

A manager says, "Go." A leader says, "Let's go."

A good comparison of management to leadership is when a manager says, "Go," a leader says, "Let's go." The virtual leader is involved in the doing. The virtual leader works side by side with those on his or her team to ensure that it works; assures that the workers are trained; and accepts responsibility for their actions.

The traditional view of management is one based on assumptions of people's powerlessness, their lack of personal vision and inability to master the forces of change. The new view of leadership will center more on the subtle and important tasks. Today's virtual leader needs to be the designer, steward, and teacher of the team and organization.

Core Competencies of Leaders

Think of a virtual leader's core competencies as character, vision, behavior, and self-confidence.

Character would be using humor and humility, and by nature be inclined to treat individuals in his or her organization equally.

Vision is when a leader can spread his or her imagination to boundaries beyond what is known today.

Behavior creates and shapes change, rather than accept it, and challenges the status quo, refusing to accept that it has never been done that way before.

Self-confidence in a leader enables that leader to have confidence in, and support the advancement of, the people in his or her organization.

Other leadership traits to be mindful of would be: a slightly nonconformist, inquisitive, action-oriented, intuitive, tenacious, open-minded to learning, candid and a network builder.

Leading People

The character and qualities that are found in successful virtual leaders are essential at all levels of responsibility.

Virtual leaders need to become leaders of change in order to have their organizations prepared for the many transitions that will take place in the virtual business world. Virtual leaders have to recognize that they have to throw aside the practices of the past in order to survive in the future. This can be seen in a story of two mice and how they responded to their cheese being moved.

Spencer Johnson's *Who Moved My Cheese* tells a delightful story of how two mice had the opportunity to adapt to change as they found their supply of cheese diminishing. One adapted to change quickly and let go of the old cheese (the old business). It enjoyed the search for a newer supply (new business). The other mouse failed to acknowledge the need for any change and suffered for it.

The virtual leadership revolution is happening now. Not tomorrow.

As a new remote leader, Kyle was one who like many of us had the basic managerial skills but needed to bridge that gap on how to lead a virtual team. Initially clueless as to what he needed, he learned how to:

- foster teamwork
- think globally
- see the value of cultural diversity
- trust enough in the team to use empowerment
- embrace shared leadership
- embrace change
- hunt for new opportunities
- demonstrate technological savvy

It is important to note how corporate visions, customer satisfaction and values are at the top of the list: fostering teamwork, thinking globally, and valuing cultural diversity. Each alone is a non-measurable but as a whole, their success could be easily understood.

The New Reality

There is a true danger that a virtual organization will have too many managers and not enough leaders. The new reality is: Both are essential. If not, entropy becomes the new infrastructure of the workplace. It will not be able to visualize a different future. Nor will it be able to make the needed changes quickly enough. It will be up to the virtual leaders of the future to bring out the best in their employees.

The questions in your mind become:
Do you want to be the last of the old generation of managers —the dinosaurs?

Or do you want to be the first of the new generation of leaders who can fulfill both roles?

Any virtual leader can survive working as a manager, but he or she can assist the organization to reach its full potential only by being a part of the new generation of leaders.

Will they stay with the old cheese or will they change as the cheese is moved?

Will they and their teams survive?

The only result that could occur would be very simple: change or fail. The choice will be theirs, but the cost will be yours. What's your choice?

**The virtual leadership revolution
is happening now. Not tomorrow.**

Ron's Takeaway

Virtual leaders are involved in the doing. They work side by side with those on their team to ensure that it works; assures that the workers are trained; and accepts responsibility for their actions. There are many books that tell you how you must be a leader to be successful— they are only part right. You must be able to be an effective manager as well. They key is to understand the differences and shift to that method if the situation calls for it.

Debates surface around the issue of leadership versus management. Is there a difference? Which are you? Are there times when you need to combine the two roles? Explore the quizzes below.

Leader vs Manager Quiz

Inc. magazine	https://bit.ly/2qhLSnA
ProProfs	https://bit.ly/2LvkzA1
Practical Management	https://bit.ly/2wk9Rrs

Virtual Nuggets

CHAPTER 8

Leading Virtual Team Meetings

The purpose is to establish a bond;
a connection that helps show that the person
at the other end of that Information Highway
is more than just a voice on the line.

One of the biggest things that Kyle had to grasp and understand was how to schedule and execute virtual team meetings. In the traditional face-to-face meetings, a lot of time is wasted. Participants don't show up at the same time; often, there isn't an agenda; and typically, they don't end when initially planned. And when the meeting is over, you walk out the door and might think: What did we accomplish? Or even: That was a waste of time.

After stumbling for a few months, Kyle figured out that he had lost everyone's attention within 30 minutes. He needed to change his ways. If he didn't, his team would be deemed a failure. He determined that the first thing he needed to tackle was to always create a plan and an agenda for each meeting going forward. When he did, he immediately noticed that interest, enthusiasm and a feeling of ownership surfaced.

What do you consider when planning a meeting?

Leading a meeting or communicating with a virtual team is a challenge. There is a very fine balance between having the right amount of information available to the team members versus crossing into information overload. Most have the tendency to over communicate by sending copies of everything to everyone on the team—that everything has to be shared with the entire team. It doesn't. As a leader, what you're doing is setting the expectation that you expect all on your team to send tons of information … no matter how relevant it is. Is that what you really want? I can tell you, it's not what your team members want.

Tips for Planning a Meeting

As the virtual leader, you set the tone and the pace. Being able to articulate an email goes a long way, of course. But on a virtual team, good communication really depends on a variety of methods that you can use.

Planning a Meeting in Different Time Zones

When you have a team that is global, different time zones will have an impact on the work day for everyone. My home base is Colorado. If I call a meeting with my team and one member is in Ireland, and another is in the Philippines and the rest scattered across the United States, I need to be extremely sensitive to the 7-hour difference that my Irish contact carries and the 15-hour difference that my Filipino member needs to work with.

If you schedule a video face time with those who aren't in your immediate time zone, think again. Taking their time into consideration is more important than yours. Determine what time ranges work for each ... then find the medium and fringe hours that will work for all.

For my regular meetings, I like to shift the time scheduling periodically because I will have one team member that's in Florida and another in California and it is very easy to intrude into their private time. Now, when you add a global component, it becomes even more interesting. It was nothing unusual for me to be up at 3 AM to have a conference call with a team member in Singapore, or 5 AM to present a class to students in India, or 10 PM evening call speaking to quality representatives in Philippines for an early afternoon call with them.

Another consideration involves establishing the right balance of personal and business interaction. Something that I believe is essential is to prime the pump—to get the communications flowing with the team. And yes, I really do have a pump in my office to remind me to do so.

I love the Zig Ziglar story from back in the 1980s on how to get to the really great water you must prime the pump first. The communication factor with any team becomes the tipping point between success and failure. You must be willing to invest your time and energy toward it so you are able to get the results you are striving for.

The FCR Virtual Leadership Method

F is for knowing the *different* **formats** *of communications,* such as email, phone calls, video conferencing, or face-to-face meetings.

C is for the *cues of* **communications** that tell you more than just words: visual, audio, body language that provide cues of how the information is being received or stress levels.

R is for the *value of* relationships—knowing your individual team members' personalities, their personal and professional goals, as well as any issues that may influence their work behavior allows you to communicate effectively and work with them.

Scheduling the Meetings

Monday is one of my favorite work days. I use two hours of it to reach out. These one-on-one times are my means to prime the pump with each team member. A matter of fact, I consider this to be one of the most critical points in communications for any manager to establish relationships, trust, and accountability.

During the Monday meetings, I do something that is alien to the majority of meetings that managers and leaders have. My meetings are not about work. I don't talk about work. I know that is hard for some not to because it is even difficult for some of my team members, but I insist that work is set aside for the short time we are talking. The purpose is to establish a bond; a connection that helps show that the person at the other end of that Information Highway is more than just a voice on the line. You want that person to understand that the only time he or she is going to hear from you isn't when you want to give him or her more work, or that the team member is in trouble.

My Monday one-on-one time is not a video chat. It is just talking on the phone—hearing about what's going on in his or her life, including house moving, redecorating, how's Johnny doing on the baseball team, or any problems that I need to understand that person is encountering outside of work. Or simply did my team member see the new movie last week. It opens up a variety of information that helps me work with each—from personal interests and goals. I want them to be successful. And you should want your team members to be successful also.

At least once a week, I use video conferencing. My personal favorite I recommend is Zoom.com, a platform I highly recommend due to its quality, ease-of-use, and I love the free price tag. Video conferencing replaces the time where people can wander into a physical conference room and just talk back and forth or meet each other at the water cooler. Suggestion: Don't jump right into the meeting subject matter and agenda. Give your participants the time and opportunity to banter back and forth—ten minutes should be ample. This socialization is important and a powerful part of a strong team.

> **Keep your time management as a critical part of *their* workday.**

Keep in mind that some may be apprehensive about discussing problems or even asking questions when others are *in the virtual room*, or may not be careful enough and express too many concerns. Or they may be concerned about how they appear on the video to the other team members. That's where a group teleconference may work better. It can "loosen" them up, gaining confidence when the camera is on.

Keep your time management as a critical part of *their* workday. Your virtual team will see that you respect the one thing that they cannot get more of—their time. Start the meeting on time, and end on time. Sometimes you, and they, may have meetings that are back-to-back. If someone starts late or runs over, expecting everybody just to sit there while he or she finishes creates frustration and stress. Neither is wanted and can be avoided.

I like to keep meetings short—under 30 minutes. After that point, the attention span for most starts declining. When attention strays, it is not uncommon for multitasking to surface—from texting, to surfing the internet, to writing emails—none of which are relevant to the meeting. You've lost your emphasis on what you expected to gain. Think of the times you've been in a group meeting, and you saw people start squirming, looking at their phones and displaying blank stares. The meeting got off track, and was extended 20 minutes without anything more having been accomplished.

Definitely have an agenda for the weekly meeting that will address a major project, program issue, performance issues, or a professional development activity that your team is involved with. If something comes up in a meeting, which looks like it may take more time, schedule another meeting and keep this one on topic.

When using a video conference, remember to make eye contact, smile and nod, making your presence personable. And remember that you're on camera—others are watching. This is not the time to blow your nose or pick your teeth. Stay fairly close to the camera so your team members can actually see you. And use mute when you're not speaking so that the background noise doesn't interfere or override the conversation. No one wants to hear your other phone ringing, the dog barking, or (if you have them) kids playing or talking.

There's nothing more frustrating than to have a large (or small) virtual meeting in progress and you hear somebody talking in the background. I've been on conference calls and heard arguing in the background. One memorable one was of a granddaughter and grandfather arguing about her bra straps showing. Two ubiquitous annoyances would be the shuffling of papers or the continual clicking of people typing into their computers.

eMail Smarts for Virtual Connecting

Email is a fantastic tool, but it shouldn't control your life. Check it regularly but don't feel that you must pick up your cell phone when you hear that ding from an email coming in. Don't get caught up in the Blackberry effect—dings come in during a meeting and all look at their phones—*is it mine?* Better yet, don't let dings come in and set a time frame when emails are checked —maybe two or three times a day. If you succumb to continuously checking your emails and texts, your productivity will be affected and your workday may need to be extended to catch up.

Imagine you are having dinner with someone you care about and the ding comes in. I can guarantee you that whoever you are with will be irritated that you care more about the phone call than him or her. Start training those who email you. In business, ask for the use of a descriptor in the subject line of incoming emails, with one of three choices: *Urgent, FYI Only,* or *Action Required by (date).* So, if urgent appears in the subject line, you know to continue. It needs your immediate response. FYI Only … ignore it. It means no action is required. And Action Required by (include date attachment/s need returning) will assist in timely replies. Using one of these in your outgoing email subject line will be a quick clarification to those on the receiving end as well.

Personally, I hate *Reply All* and do not use it myself. Some companies have gone to the point where they are automatically deactivating the "reply all" function. Why? Because it overloads many email systems. For me, there's nothing more irritating than to get 20 to 30 emails … all that *okay, thank you*, etc. I get it, sometimes it's a CYA (cover your ass). If that's the case, do a direct email and leave the others out. If it's important, copy that person and ask yourself, *does anyone else really need to know this?* If you do forward it to others, be sure to tell them why and if any action is required on their part.

> Don't send an angry, or insulting, response as if it was a SCUD missile

And, if you do send a reply all, give everybody the same information. Do not include everybody's attachments—they all got them on the first go around.

Writing emails is important and I take extra care in creating them. With virtual teams, there isn't the physical "water cooler conversation" with another to talk things over. Before I respond, I make an effort to understand his or her point or concern. Because he or she took the time to email me, it must be important. So, I don't want to misinterpret what this person was saying. And I don't want to send an angry, or insulting, response as if it was a SCUD missile. If it's something that is really important, pick up the phone and call directly. A short phone call can save a ton of energy and maybe save a situation from escalating and going south on you.

If you have a large virtual team, you need to keep an updated list of your team members' email addresses, contact information, birthdays, etc. Do take care and remove those who have been transferred or terminated and add new hires.

Being on a virtual team can generate a lot of unintentional or unimportant traffic. Staying on top of it can be exhausting, frustrating, and cause levels of stress at home. And it is unnecessary. Work with the team to find the right balance by promoting communications that build motivation and support within the team—a positive environment. While email is a great tool, it doesn't match the emotional connection that you get with visual interaction with the other team members. Encourage them to connect directly with each other. Give them the capability of having their own Zoom accounts. They can hold a short (or long) meeting, share screens—they can even record what they do. And at same time, you will be able to reduce the number of committee meetings that become demotivators.

Use different formats for updating status and giving those brief reports. I use a monthly scorecard for every member on my team, using an Excel spreadsheet for each. I developed a basic format where they can fill in their information and it is shared with the entire team. This enables me to learn who is doing what and I can visually see if our project is on track. At the same time, I note where help may be needed and any possible learning opportunities I can incorporate. All that will be revealed in my next book, *Virtual Accountability How to Use Scorecarding to Track Performance, and Recognize the Early Warning Signals.*

If you get the impression that someone is pushing back deadlines or not fulfilling the responsibilities of the job he or she was hired to do, never address it in a weekly video conference. And don't address it on the Monday one-on-one time. Instead, schedule a separate one-on-one video conference. The reason why I recommend including video and not via phone (and definitely not email), is that you want you to be visually connected—seeing his or her face and body language. Make sure that your expectations are understood and that the resources are available to get the job done. This is definitely uncomfortable when you are questioning a virtual team member's inadequate job performance. Afterward I always followed up with an email which summarized my interpretation of the meeting and my expectations.

Ron's Takeaway

Being a virtual leader means that you need to rely on having good lines of communication. It also means you are at risk of information overload. Trying to stay on top of everything can be frustrating and even cause problems at home (this is from experience). You have many roles to fill in your life—meaning you must learn how to use technology to your best advantage. You will be happier, your team will be less stressed, and your family life will be much more fulfilling.

As a pilot watches all those indicators in their cockpit, they are not looking as much for those that are showing no issues, but they are watching for those that show a problem or something that needs their attention. You must do the same—spend your time looking for those early warning signals that need your attention and do not worry about those others. If they end up needing your attention, believe me, they will let you know.

There are a variety of remote meeting options. Most know about Skype. Below are several you may not be aware of.

Team Meeting Options

Big Blue Button	BigBlueButton.org open sourced real-time sharing of audio, video, slides, live chat. Great for teachers and instructors
Web Huddle	WebHuddle.com open source. Free. Host up to 10 attendees
Meeting Burner	MeetingBurner.com up to 10 attendees for free. Screen share. Works with iPhones, iPads, Android phones
Zoho Meeting	Zoho.com up to 5 participants for free. $8 per month up to 100 participants
Zoom	Zoom.us free for unlimited number of meetings up to 100 participants (40 minutes per meeting)
Any Meeting	AnyMeeting.com ad-based but free to users. Up to 200 attendees, screen sharing, recording

CHAPTER 9

This End is Just the Beginning of the Virtual Nuggets Series

Be mindful that management skills
will only come with experience.

As we come to the end of the first book in the Virtual Nuggets Series, my personal goal was for you to see that it can actually be fun being the virtual leader that every organization needs. In our role as leaders, we have a fantastic opportunity to not only help our organizations be successful in their business ventures but to provide the support for our team members so that they can achieve the goals and objectives that they have set for themselves.

Although being a leader in a virtual environment is tough, you were selected for the position because you have the knowledge and skills to be successful. If you are not in a management position yet, you are wise to be looking ahead and acquiring all the professional management knowledge you can. But, be mindful that management skills will only come with experience.

Managing any team is a tough job. The virtual leader must face two additional challenges. The first is not being in the same city, the same state, or even the same country as your team members. The second is that he may be contending with a vast array of time zones making scheduling conference calls and video conferencing a major headache, if not a nightmare.

Personally, I consider the Belbin Team Roles as one of the best kept secrets in the United States. It is time to get the word out about what a fantastic tool it can be for the virtual team. There will be more details in a later book, and I want to stress here that this is just an introduction and not a full understanding of what took Dr. Belbin decades to develop and refine. And please, do not rely on a free survey on the internet, but rather visit those that have completed the accreditation program and have access to the extensive database. There is a risk in doing a self-assessment because you may see yourself differently than those with whom you work.

Team members who have an opportunity to meet face-to-face occasionally perform better and can reduce or distill any possible hostility in many cases. Because of the challenges of virtual leadership, it is critical to make that personal bond.

Leaders and managers use technology for video conferences, accountability, and communications, but technology is no substitute for being a good leader or manager. The problems and speed bumps that you'll encounter can be managed by understanding your leadership style and what works best for your team members using good management methods. You have a great opportunity to learn how to use all of the technology, learn to assign areas of specialization to the most qualified team members, and develop your own leadership style to help team members reach their full potential. This is why I impress upon you to prime that pump. Always remember: Before you get to those really good results, you need to invest some of yourself to make that virtual connection.

I love working with many different tools and techniques. So can you. Building trust and earning the respect of your team members is not easy—but it is so rewarding. I hope by sharing my knowledge and experiences, you can see how exciting and fantastic it is to be a virtual leader.

Dr. Ronald Beach

Ron Beach is a speaker, trainer, professor, and proud United States Marine Corps Veteran.

As the Program Chair for the Ashford University Forbes School of Business Bachelor of Business Administration degree program, he conducts classes globally from his office in Colorado to a balcony room on a cruise ship. Dr. Beach believes in staying connected with his team—no matter where he is or where his team members are.

Earning his PhD and master's degrees in Organization and Management (with an emphasis in Leadership) from Capella University, and a BLS in Liberal Studies from the University of Oklahoma, he brings his breadth of over 30 years of corporate experience as the Senior Director of US Manufacturing for a billion dollar a year electronic data storage division and was a United States Marine electronic countermeasures technician supporting operations in Laos and Cambodia during the Vietnam War.

Being an Organizational Sociologist, Dr. Beach is one of a very small number from North America who has traveled to Cambridge,

England, and earned the highly coveted Belbin Team Role Assessment Certification.

When not working with his remote teams, you might find him scuba diving, serving as a Colorado State Baldridge Examiner, or a Quality Matters Reviewer. Spare time finds him pursuing his quest as a Titanic history buff.

He resides in the beautiful state of Colorado with his wife Wendy.

Ron Beach Consults and Speaks...

Would You Like to Listen ... Learn ... Be a Stronger Leader?

Ron Beach would be delighted to participate in your Management or Human Resource conference. He is also available to speak to your group or organization. For Virtual Leadership and management consulting, email or call his office. If you want a highly interactive, informative and fun presentation or workshop, call or email him for availability.

Workshops and Keynotes Include:

Virtual Leadership | Belbin Team Roles | Decision Making with Statistics | Corporate Ethics Safety in the Workplace | Japanese Production Systems | Use of Teams and Group Dynamics | Utilizing Project Management International Leadership | Leadership Trends of the Next Decade | Global Supply Chain Management

Consulting by the Hour or by the Project

You want information and resources to help your organization with virtual leadership develop. My blogs are available and social media accounts are right up your alley in supplying information for today's virtual leader. Let's get connected:

Ron@RonaldBeach.com | 720/202-0141

WEBSITES

TheRonaldBeach.com

RonaldBeach.com

RonaldBeach.info

SOCIAL MEDIA

 @DrRonaldBeach

 Dr.RonaldBeach

 Ronald Beach

BOOK TWO OF THE VIRTUAL NUGGETS SERIES

VIRTUAL
ACCOUNTABILITY

How to Use Scorecarding to Track Performance, and Recognize the Early Warning Signals

CHAPTER 1

GETTING READY YOUR VIRTUAL MUSCLE

Most don't like to handle problems.

Kyle has made significant strides in his management and the team is doing fantastic. The problem is how to keep an eye on the so many little things before they become big issues. How should he handle a performance issue? When should he handle it? And are there any pitfalls that he should be on alert for?

Let's think of a small problem with a remote member on Kyle's team as being a glass with a small amount of water in it. If the problem is the water itself and it is handled right away, it is not an issue. Contrary to the belief and practice of many, the size of the problem doesn't matter. What is critical is how long before you see the problem and address it. If you hold the glass for a minute before taking care of the problem, it is not a problem. If you wait an hour, you begin to feel the strain of the muscles in your arm. If you wait a day, the muscles start to become numb. The amount of water has not changed (the size of the problem) but it is the length of time before you take care of it.

Most don't like to handle problems. Why? Simply because they are not the fun part of the job. But handling them is one of the most important things you do as a manager. There are two essential elements to performance issues in a virtual team:

1. When you see the problem; and

2. How long before you address it.

Throughout *Virtual Accountability*, I will show you how to use the scorecard concept to get the early warnings of a performance issue and then how to address it before it causes the project to derail.